I0521035

Well, That Was Enlightening

Well, That Was Enlightening

Katie Simpson

Copyright

Well, That Was Enlightening
© 2025 Katherine Simpson

All rights reserved. No part of this book may be reproduced, stored in a retrieval system, or transmitted in any form or by any means — electronic, mechanical, photocopying, recording, or otherwise — without the prior written permission of the publisher, except for brief quotations used in reviews or critical articles.

This is a work of nonfiction. Names, details, and identifying characteristics may have been changed to protect privacy. Any resemblance to actual persons, living or dead, is entirely coincidental.

Published in the United States by Ember & Oak Consulting LLC dba Ember & Oak Press, Montana. For inquires visit www.katiesimpsonbooks.com.

ISBN: 979-8-9936949-0-0
Cover design by Katie Simpson
Printed in the United States of America

First Edition

Dedication

For Ken. Always.

Because somehow, love found its way through chaos, sarcasm, and still came out holy.

Disclaimer

This book is based on my personal experiences, observations, and reflections. It is not a substitute for professional advice, therapy, or medical treatment.

The thoughts and opinions expressed here are my own and reflect my understanding of life, spirituality, and personal growth at the time of writing. Names and identifying details have been changed or omitted to protect privacy.

If something you read here helps you, I'm grateful.
If something challenges you, I hope you sit with it.
Either way, take what serves your soul and leave the rest for someone else's lesson.

Acknowledgments

To the Universe — for your terrible timing, impeccable humor, and endless patience while I figured it out.

To my husband, Ken — thank you for being my steady ground, my comic relief, and my proof that love doesn't need conditions or ceremonies to be sacred. You've seen every version of me and stayed anyway.

To my children — thank you for giving me reasons to keep growing, even when it hurt. Every chapter of my life has been written with you in mind.

To my friends who showed up while I was rebuilding — you know who you are. Thank you for your honesty, laughter, and coffee deliveries.

To every reader who has ever questioned what they were taught, wondered if they were broken, or looked up at the sky and said, "Really, Universe?" — this one's for you.

And finally, to the version of me who kept getting back up even when she didn't know how. I see you. I'm so proud of you.

Preface

I didn't set out to write a book about spirituality. Honestly, I set out to survive.

For most of my life, I did what I was told. I followed the rules, checked the boxes, tried to earn love through obedience and achievement. I spent years believing God was keeping score and that I was constantly coming up short.

Then everything I thought I knew fell apart. My religion. My marriage. My sense of identity. The life I'd built on "shoulds" crumbled and for the first time, I was forced to ask the one question that changed everything:

What if the problem wasn't me? What if the system was broken?

That question cracked everything open.

What followed wasn't a straight path to enlightenment. It was messy, painful, funny, and full of detours. I went to therapy that didn't help. I tried to pray my way through trauma that needed action, not penance. I chased peace through self-help books and still ended up ugly-crying on the kitchen floor.

And somewhere in the middle of all that chaos, I started hearing something quieter. A voice that didn't sound like judgment, but truth. It told me that maybe I wasn't lost. Maybe I was being rerouted.

This book is about that reroute. The one that takes you from control to surrender, from religion to relationship, from fear to freedom.

It's about realizing the Universe isn't testing you; it's teaching you. That spirituality doesn't have to be branded, restricted, or mediated. It can be personal, irreverent, funny, and still holy.

I wrote this book for anyone who's ever felt disillusioned, disappointed, or spiritually homeless. For anyone who's ever whispered, "If this is what faith feels like, I must be doing it wrong."

You're not. You're just waking up.

I hope these pages make you laugh, cry, and most importantly, feel seen. I hope they remind you that you don't have to have it all figured out to be growing, you just have to keep going.

So pour some coffee (or wine, no judgment), take a deep breath, and settle in.

This isn't a sermon. It's a conversation. A messy, honest one about how life falls apart, and how maybe, just maybe, that's where the light finally gets in.

Note to the Reader

Before you dive in, I want to be clear about something: this isn't a book *against* any religion. It's not about proving anyone wrong or dismantling belief; it's about *expanding* it.

If faith, prayer, church, or any form of worship brings you peace, keep it. Truly. The world needs more people who feel grounded in love.

This book is about thinking outside the box. The one that says there's only one "right" way to connect with the divine. It's about loosening the rules we've been handed and asking, *What if there's more?*

What if God, Source, the Universe — whatever name you use — has been speaking to you all along, in ways you were never taught to recognize?

I share my story not to convince you to believe what I believe, but to remind you that you don't need permission to question what doesn't feel right for you. You're allowed to explore. You're allowed to wonder. You're allowed to evolve.

This isn't a guidebook or a sermon. It's a conversation about growth, resilience, humor, and the quiet, stubborn light that keeps us going even when everything else falls apart.

As you read, take what resonates and leave what doesn't. Let curiosity lead the way. My hope is that these pages help you feel a little less alone, a little more seen, and a lot more open to the possibility that life, in all its chaos and beauty, is still working for your highest good.

Table of Contents

Chapter 1 – Welcome to Earth School

You didn't sign up for this class — or did you?

I started questioning my reason for existing when I was a young child. Something about life always seemed… off to me. Even then, I could sense that something wasn't adding up. Why did we come here to suffer? Why was life so hard and people so awful to each other? I didn't want that for me. I wanted more.

There were moments when I'd sit alone, staring out a window or lying in the grass, and I'd feel this strange ache like homesickness for a place I couldn't name. I had these distant, dreamlike memories of a life that felt softer, full of love, freedom, and kindness. But where were those memories coming from? I couldn't explain it, but I knew deep down that this world wasn't the whole story. It was like my soul remembered something my body had forgotten.

That quiet wondering never went away. It just learned to whisper instead of shout. Somewhere deep inside, I think I always knew we come here already whole and then spend a lifetime trying to remember that truth.

Have you ever looked around at your life and thought, *Is this it?* The bills, the chores, the endless cycle of coffee, chaos, and questionable decisions. Somewhere between chasing promotions, raising kids, or just trying to keep our sanity intact, we forget that life isn't supposed to be a treadmill. We're not here just to survive it; we're supposed to learn something from it.

At least, that's what I tell myself when things go sideways. Which, to be clear, is often. Because if there isn't a deeper purpose to all of this, then honestly, what's the point?

Most of us were handed some kind of belief system as kids. Maybe you went to church on holidays. Maybe you were baptized before you could hold your own head up. Maybe, like me, you grew up in a religion that claimed God loved you unconditionally, so long as you followed a list of conditions.

In my world, God's approval felt like trying to win Employee of the Month at the universe's most judgmental corporation. There were rules for everything: what to wear, how to pray, who to marry, how to think. It was like cosmic micromanagement with eternal consequences. I was told that obedience equaled salvation and questioning anything meant rebellion.

And I've always been terrible at obedience.

Somewhere along the way, I realized I didn't need a middleman to translate my prayers. I didn't need someone standing between me and the Divine, deciding whether my messy, human self was worthy of love. I figured if God is love, then love doesn't need a permission slip.

That realization didn't come from a sermon. It came from surviving from heartbreaks that gutted me, losses that rearranged me, and the quiet moments when I was sure no one was listening, yet somehow, I still felt guided. It came from the small miracles that showed up between the big disasters.

And in those moments of quiet guidance, I sometimes caught a faint echo of that childhood memory. That feeling of home, of something vast and kind that existed before rules or judgment. It was the same feeling, just remembered in grown-up language.

So maybe we did sign up for this class. Maybe before we landed here (complete with taxes, Amazon returns, and emotional baggage), we agreed to learn something about what it means to be human. Maybe Earth is less a punishment and more a practical workshop for souls who thought they could handle it. (Joke's on us.)

What if every frustration, every delay, every heartbreak is a pop quiz designed to remind us who we really are? Not the roles we play, not the rules we inherited, but the raw truth underneath all the noise.

The problem is the lessons aren't labeled. There's no syllabus, no warning that today's meltdown is tomorrow's enlightenment. Growth sneaks in wearing the disguise of disappointment. Healing feels like chaos before it feels like peace.

And yet, somewhere in all that mess, something sacred is happening.

Maybe our purpose isn't to figure it all out. Maybe it's to show up anyway and to keep learning, keep laughing, and keep finding pieces of meaning in the middle of the absurd. Maybe the goal isn't perfection but participation.

So welcome to Earth School. The tuition is steep, the homework is relentless, and the exams are unannounced. But the lessons?

They're life-changing, if you're brave enough to stay awake for them.

I learned early that religion can be a master class in contradiction. On one hand, you're told God is love. On the other, you're warned, "He's keeping receipts." It's like being raised by a parent who says, "I adore you," while holding a clipboard of your screwups.

In my house, church wasn't optional. Sundays weren't for sleeping in or coffee runs. They were for hymns, starched clothes, and sermons that promised grace, if you could earn it. We were taught that joy was suspicious, curiosity was dangerous, and questioning the rules meant you were on a slippery slope straight to eternal damnation. (I was probably halfway down that slope by age twelve.)

What I remember most, though, wasn't the fire-and-brimstone. It was the quiet confusion. Because even as a kid, something inside me whispered, *this can't be it.*

If God is as big and loving as they say, why would He need such fragile humans to defend His rules? Why would unconditional love come with so many conditions?

I kept those questions tucked away, mostly because asking them out loud was like lighting a match in a room full of gas fumes. So, I did what good girls do. I smiled, nodded, memorized the verses, and pretended I didn't feel like an imposter.

But pretending has an expiration date.

My first real rebellion wasn't loud or dramatic, it was quiet. It was me sitting in a pew one Sunday, looking around at the sea of forced smiles and realizing I didn't feel God there. I felt judgment, guilt, and performance, but not presence. It hit me like a truth bomb I couldn't unhear. *This isn't what love feels like.*

That moment cracked something open in me. I didn't know it then, but that's where my spiritual life began. Not in obedience but in curiosity. I wanted to find the real thing. Not the version filtered through fear or hierarchy. But the raw, intimate, unpolished kind of faith that shows up in heartbreak, in laughter, in the way the sunset makes you feel both tiny and infinite all at once.

Leaving religion wasn't easy. You don't just walk away from a belief system. You unlearn it one guilt trip at a time. Every time I skipped church, some internal voice whispered, *You're backsliding.* (Backsliding, by the way, is church-speak for "*heading down the wrong path.*")

It took years to untangle that conditioning. The idea that love had prerequisites or that spirituality belonged to someone else's rulebook. But every loss, every heartbreak, every "what now?" moment became a teacher. Each one stripped away another layer of falsehood until all that was left was something beautifully simple: my own connection.

And that connection, that small, steady voice inside, felt eerily familiar. It was the same voice I'd known as a child when I remembered that other place, the one filled with love and freedom. Maybe those weren't random memories after all. Maybe they were breadcrumbs.

It's funny how the Universe works. The more I stopped chasing "the right way" to believe, the more peace I found. The less I begged for answers, the more I noticed signs. Little winks from the divine tucked inside ordinary days.

Now, I don't picture God as some cosmic referee in the sky. To me, God is that quiet knowing when the world goes still. God is the laughter that bubbles up when everything feels heavy. God is the way people show up right when you need them most.

If you strip away all the noise, the doctrine, and the fear, what's left is connection. The reminder that we're all part of something infinitely bigger (and funnier) than we realize.

So maybe, just maybe, this class we didn't sign up for is teaching us exactly what we came here to remember:
That love doesn't require perfection.
That faith doesn't require a middleman.
And that maybe enlightenment isn't about rising above being human, it's about embracing it.

Because, let's be honest, if there's a test at the end of this, I'm still not sure I'm passing. But I'm showing up, I'm learning, and I'm laughing.

And for now, that's enough.

Chapter 2 – The Universe Doesn't Take Suggestions

When I first started trying to heal from everything I'd been through, I thought the smart thing to do was to go to therapy. That's what you're supposed to do, right? I sat in several offices, pouring my heart out, rehashing the same story over and over again. The pain, the betrayal, the guilt.

The problem was, every time I left, I felt worse. I wasn't healing. I was reliving. Each session reopened the wound, and instead of processing the pain, I was just memorizing it.

At one point, I remember thinking, *Is this it?* Is healing just talking about your trauma until your voice gives out?

So I decided to do what I've always done best -- figure it out myself.

I started reading everything I could get my hands on about healing, spirituality, energy, and consciousness. And that's when I stumbled across something that shook me to my core, not in the "hallelujah" kind of way, but in the "my-entire-belief-system-is-crumbling" kind of way.

I learned the truth about my religion.

The institution I'd trusted my entire life, the one that told me how to think, dress, love, and even drink, was built on manipulation, control, and fear. I'd been told it was divine truth. Turns out it was a very human system created by a man whose behavior was, let's just say, questionable at best.

The deeper I dug, the worse it got. Story after story from credible, intelligent people. People who had once been leaders, scholars, believers, all telling the same tale. They had left because they'd discovered the truth.

I felt sick. Deceived. Heartbroken.

It wasn't just about the lies. It was about the years I'd spent living small to earn love that was supposed to be unconditional. I had been terrified to think for myself because I believed disobedience meant damnation.

I remember sitting on the edge of my bed one night, staring at the wall, and realizing that *I don't need a middleman to talk to God.*

That was the first real moment of freedom.

At first, it didn't feel empowering. It felt terrifying. The old conditioning doesn't just fall away. It clings. It whispers. It tells you that independence is arrogance, that doubt is rebellion. My mind would ping-pong between fear and relief like I was detoxing from spiritual caffeine.

But little by little, I started to test it.

I stopped asking permission to trust my own intuition.
I started making decisions based on peace, not guilt.
I quit begging the Universe to listen to me and started listening to it instead.

And that's when things began to shift.

For the first time in my life, I wasn't praying to some faraway robe wearing God in the clouds. I was listening inward, to the quiet, steady knowing that had always lived inside me. It didn't sound like the sermons or the scriptures. It wasn't booming or dramatic. It was soft, calm, and honest. And I realized that what I'd been calling "God" all those years might have been this voice all along.

That realization was both comforting and disorienting. Because if God wasn't *out there*, then He was *in here*. And if He was in here, then maybe I'd never been lost, just disconnected.

When I say *Universe*, I don't mean it as a trendy stand-in for God or some cosmic Pinterest quote about manifesting your dream life. I mean *everything*.

The energy that runs through all of us. The divine intelligence that connects love, grief, timing, laughter — all of it.

To me, the Universe *is* God. It's Source, Spirit, whatever name helps you breathe when life doesn't make sense. I use "Universe" because it feels big enough to hold it all — the sacred, the scientific, the funny, the brutal. It doesn't exclude God; it expands Him. It's not about rejecting faith. It's about realizing the Divine isn't limited to one language, one religion, or one building. It's everywhere. Speaking in signs, synchronicities, and those tiny gut nudges we keep trying to rationalize away.

And once you start paying attention to it, it's like someone turns the volume up on your own life.

I've learned the Universe doesn't take suggestions. You can plead, plan, and make vision boards all day long, but it's going to unfold in the way that serves your growth, not your convenience.

And if you're anything like me, that's maddening.

I used to think that if I just prayed hard enough or "manifested" correctly, I could skip the messy parts of growth. Turns out, the Universe has no interest in skipping steps. It's not punishing us, it's preparing us.

When you stop fighting what is and start asking what it's teaching you, everything changes.

The same energy that once broke me started guiding me. I realized that my intuition, that quiet, steady voice I'd been trained to ignore, had been speaking truth the whole time. It wasn't loud or dramatic. It didn't demand or threaten. It whispered.

And every time I listened, things got a little lighter. A little clearer.

The Universe, I've learned, doesn't work like a vending machine. You don't punch in your order and wait for your miracle to drop. It's more like a GPS. It gives you the next turn, not the whole map.

And yeah, sometimes you miss a turn. But that's okay. The route recalculates.

Now, when things don't go my way, I don't panic like I used to. I pause, breathe, and think, *Okay, Universe. I get it. You're steering.*

I may not always like where it's taking me, but I've learned to trust that it knows the terrain better than I do.

So yes, the Universe doesn't take suggestions.

It takes alignment.

And when you finally stop arguing with it, life stops feeling like a punishment and starts feeling like a partnership.

Chapter 3 – Religious Trauma & Other Holy Hangovers

When I first met Ken, I was still knee-deep in religious recovery. Equal parts hopeful and haunted. I thought I was "healing," but really, I was still trying to pass a final exam in a class I should've dropped years ago.

The religion I'd left behind had trained me well. Smile through the pain, suppress your doubts, and for God's sake, save everyone else while you're at it. So naturally, when I met this calm, grounded, maddeningly logical man, my first instinct wasn't just to love him — it was to save him.

I was convinced he needed my religion. I'd been taught that spreading "truth" was an act of love, so I turned our early relationship into a low-key missionary project. I shared pamphlets, scriptures, and testimonies. I probably would've hosted a baptism in the kitchen sink if he'd stood still long enough.

Ken, bless him, never mocked me or argued. He'd just listen, let me talk, and then in his steady way say, "I don't do organized religion. I'll support you, but that's not my path."

At first, I took it as a challenge. My brain said, *He just hasn't seen the light yet.* My heart said, *He already has, and it's not the kind that flickers under a stained-glass window.*

Over time, something started to shift. I found myself confiding in him. Whispering the questions I wasn't supposed to ask out loud. Why did God's love come with so many rules? Why did a "faith built on grace" feel so conditional? Why did I feel more peace sitting by the river with him than I ever had sitting in a pew?

Ken would just listen, really listen, and never once try to fix me. That alone was disarming. Someone simply letting me exist in my uncertainty. One night, I told him how terrified I was that even questioning my old faith would send me straight to eternal damnation.

He looked at me, calm, steady, no judgment, and said, "Didn't they already excommunicate you based on lies? Didn't they sweep the abuse you went through under the carpet? Didn't they tell you that you were the problem?"

"Yes," I said quietly.

He raised an eyebrow. "Then why in God's name would you ever want to go back?"

And there it was.

That one sentence hit harder than every sermon I'd ever sat through. It snapped the spell. I realized how completely brainwashed I'd been. How deeply fear had rewired my logic. I'd been begging for forgiveness from people who'd already written me off. Trying to earn redemption from a system that never believed I was worthy in the first place.

The more distance I got, the more I began to see the pattern. In my old religion, men weren't trained clergy, they were "called." One day, a layman would be chosen and suddenly become a bishop, the spiritual head of hundreds of people. No theology degree. No counseling experience. No training in how to handle abuse or trauma. Just a handshake, a title, and the belief that he now spoke for God.

Because only married men could qualify, their wives were automatically elevated too. Unofficially sainted by association. Together, they became the power couple of the congregation, positioned to guide everyone else. What could possibly go wrong?

Everything.

In my case, the bishop was a young man and a friend of my ex-husband. And, as you might guess, friendship won out over fairness. He believed every word my ex said about me. He didn't care that there were police reports to back up my stories of abuse. He never asked for my side. Instead, he inserted himself into our custody dispute, certain that his personal feelings were "divine revelation."

And just like that, he had the power to destroy me and he used it. He saw to it that I was excommunicated.

Why? Because in that system, personal bias wrapped in scripture was considered holy judgment. Truth didn't matter. Evidence didn't matter. The only thing that mattered was authority and maintaining it.

That's how it happens. The moment you tell people they can't question leadership, abuse of power stops being a possibility and becomes a guarantee.

And that's exactly what broke me open. Because I finally saw what had been hiding in plain sight. The system wasn't built on love; it was built on control. A hierarchy pretending to be humility. A structure that confused obedience with holiness and silence with faith.

For the first time, I saw my own reflection clearly; not as someone broken or unworthy, but as someone who had been tricked into believing she was.

Ken didn't give me faith; he helped me rediscover it. Real faith. The kind that doesn't require intermediaries, rituals, or approval. The kind that trusts the quiet, intuitive knowing that whispers, *You are loved exactly as you are.*

One of the hardest parts of walking away wasn't the rules; it was the people. Especially family. In my old church, family wasn't just family; it was forever. They even had ceremonies that sealed you together "for time and all eternity." Sounds comforting until you're the one left out of the eternal group photo.

When my family chose to go through that sealing ceremony without me, it hit like a gut punch. The message was clear. My absence was justified because I no longer fit their version of salvation. In their eyes, I wasn't part of the forever package anymore.

I told myself I was fine, but I wasn't. I grieved like someone had died, because in a way, something had. The bond I thought was unconditional suddenly came with spiritual paperwork I couldn't sign.

Over time, I started to see the twisted irony of it all. If eternal love can be revoked by a ceremony, was it ever love to begin with? Why would a divine, all-loving Creator need a bureaucratic process to keep families together?

That's when I realized those ceremonies weren't about love; they were about control. Love doesn't exile. Love doesn't make you earn your seat at the table.

Now, I can see it differently. Families, biological or chosen, are classrooms. Some are gentle teachers; others hand you the syllabus from hell. Either way, they're part of the lesson plan. Everyone shows up to teach you something about yourself: your strength, your boundaries, your capacity to forgive, your willingness to let go.

It's okay not to want to be "sealed" forever to people who can't see your worth. Love them, learn from them, and release them. Forever isn't meant to be forced.

I used to think God lived in church walls. Now I think He lives in laughter that returns after silence. In the way the sun hits the field behind our house just before dusk. In the simple act of being seen by someone who doesn't flinch when you finally tell the truth.

Love, I've learned, doesn't shrink you to fit its mold. It stretches to hold who you really are.

Religion gave me fear; love gave me freedom. And the Universe, in its divine irony, used a man who wanted nothing to do with organized faith to teach me what spiritual partnership actually looks like.

These days, I don't measure holiness in attendance records or scripture memorization. I measure it in peace, and in laughter, and in how quickly I can forgive myself when I mess up again (which, to be clear, is often).

I still have moments when the old programming creeps in, that whisper that says I'll never be "enough." But now, I just smile and say, "Thanks for your input," and carry on.

Because if there's one thing the Universe has made abundantly clear, it's this: love doesn't require a middleman, and redemption doesn't come from rules.

It comes from finally remembering that you were never damned, just distracted.

And maybe that's the real enlightenment. Realizing that the voice inside you, the one that whispered as a little girl that something about life felt off, was never wrong. It was never rebellion. It was remembering. Even then, you were hearing the truth beneath the noise. You just hadn't learned to trust it yet.

Chapter 4 – When the Universe Sends People as Lessons (and Some as Warnings)

Some are blessings. Some are "never again."

There are people who drift through your life like soft background music; pleasant, temporary, harmless. And then there are the ones who kick the damn door open, rearrange your furniture, and burn the house down on their way out.

My first marriage was the latter.

At the time, I thought I was marrying for forever. I believed in the story I'd been told that love was a reward for good behavior, that marriage was a sacred covenant you never walked away from, and that enduring misery somehow equaled virtue. None of that turned out to be true.

Looking back, I can see that the whole thing wasn't about punishment, it was about awakening. I just didn't know it yet.

That relationship stripped me bare. It was the kind of experience that doesn't just break your heart; it breaks your identity. Every piece of who I thought I was got scattered across that battlefield. The people-pleaser, the fixer, the "good wife," the one who thought if I could just love harder, it would all make sense.

It didn't.

I was so broken I could barely find words for what was happening inside me. There was no part of my life untouched by his control. Financial, emotional, spiritual, all controlled. And every time I tried to ask for help, it felt like shouting into a void.

But I did ask. Over and over. I would beg God for a way out, not because I wanted to give up, but because I genuinely didn't know how to leave. I had no job. No money. No independence. I was completely dependent on the same man who was destroying me.

I know it might sound strange, praying for a way out of a marriage when your entire belief system says marriage is forever. But what do you do when "forever" starts to feel like a life sentence?

I can still hear his threats. The smug certainty when he'd say, "If you ever leave me, I'll burn everything to the ground before I let you take a dime. You'll have nothing."

He meant it.

And that's the thing about living in fear, you start believing it's your destiny.

For a long time, I thought maybe I deserved it. That maybe this was the punishment for not being "righteous enough." But deep down, I kept praying. I begged for a way out that wouldn't destroy my kids or myself. I asked for a sign, for mercy, for something, anything, that looked like hope.

And then one day, Ken showed up.

He didn't ride in on a white horse or rescue me with grand gestures. He just *appeared*. Quietly. Calmly. Like the Universe had finally whispered, *You've had enough. Here's your lifeline.*

At first, I didn't recognize it. I thought he was just a kind man who listened better than most. But there was something familiar about him, something I couldn't name at the time. I didn't feel like I was meeting him; I felt like I was remembering him.

And I know how that sounds — dramatic, mystical, maybe a little ridiculous — but I believe it with everything in me. I believe Ken and I have a connection that stretches beyond this life. That we've met before, in some other time, in some other place, and promised each other we'd find our way back.

Because when I look back at the wreckage of that first marriage, I don't just see pain. I see a long chain of moments that led me straight to him. Every heartbreak, every sleepless night, every desperate prayer, all of it was leading me here.

That's what I mean when I say the Universe sends people as lessons. Sometimes, the lesson is about survival. Sometimes, it's about awakening. And if you're lucky, one of those lessons shows up as love that doesn't demand your destruction first.

Ken didn't just love me back to life, he helped me remember who I was before I forgot. The woman buried under fear and guilt and "shoulds." The one who still believed in magic, even when she was too tired to look for it.

Would I choose to go through that first marriage again?
Absolutely not.

Did I need to? Probably.

Because that version of me, the one on her knees, begging for a way out, was the most honest I'd ever been. She stopped performing. She surrendered. And in that surrender, she cracked open just enough for the light to finally get in.

Now, years later, I can say something I never thought I would. My first marriage was one of my greatest teachers. It taught me what love is *not*. It taught me what happens when you abandon yourself to keep someone else comfortable. It taught me that devotion without boundaries isn't holy, it's self-erasure.

But maybe the most important lesson it taught me was this. Sometimes the people who hurt you most aren't villains, they're volunteers. Souls who agreed, before either of you got here, to play the role that would break you open so your light could finally escape.

That doesn't mean it was okay. It just means it was meaningful.

I can't say I'm grateful for the pain exactly, but I am grateful for what it revealed. That I am stronger than I ever imagined. That real love never asks you to disappear, and that sometimes the Universe uses wreckage as an invitation.

Would I choose it again? No.
Did it save me anyway? Yes.

Because when the Universe finally sent me Ken, it wasn't to fix me. It was to remind me that I was never broken in the first place.

And that's the quiet miracle of it all. Sometimes the help you pray for doesn't arrive as lightning or revelation. Sometimes it walks into your life wearing work boots and patience. Sometimes it shows up as the soul who promised to find you when the lesson was over — not to save you, but to stand beside you while you remember you were the answer all along.

Chapter 5 – Growth Looks a Lot Like Falling Apart

Here's a quote about growth no one puts on a coffee mug - It's Awful.

Growth is exhausting, confusing, and deeply uncomfortable. You question everything — your choices, your worth, your sanity, your purpose — all while trying to hold your life together with duct tape and prayer.

Everyone loves the idea of transformation, but no one talks about how much it hurts to shed your skin. Growth sounds poetic until you're sobbing on the floor, ugly-crying into a pile of laundry, wondering why you ever asked the Universe for "lessons."

After my first marriage ended, I told myself I was healing. What I was actually doing was unraveling. Every belief I'd ever held, every illusion I'd ever clung to, started crumbling. Like the Universe had decided to knock over every emotional Jenga block just to see what I was made of.

There were days I felt like I was floating outside of myself, watching my life burn down in slow motion. I wanted to fast-forward past the pain, skip the middle, and get to the part where everything made sense again. Unfortunately, that's not how healing works.

Healing doesn't ask for your permission. It shows up, grabs a hammer, and starts dismantling everything false, no warning, no anesthetic.

When I finally left the church for good, it wasn't with a quiet exit or a whisper of doubt, it was with an *epic letter.* Years of silence and submission poured out of me in one defiant act of clarity. I put every ounce of truth I had into that letter. The hypocrisy, the manipulation, the heartbreak, the courage it took to say, *I'm done.*

And when I hit send, I could finally breathe again.

It wasn't peace at first, it was oxygen. That first gasp of freedom after holding your breath for decades.

Of course, the messages still came. There were people inside the church I'd once called friends who reached out "with love" — their words dipped in sugar, their tone dripping with pity. They'd say things like, *"You know, the only chance you have for salvation is to return."*

I remember one particular conversation with a co-worker who said that exact thing. She looked at me with this deep, earnest concern, like she was trying to save me from myself.

I thought about it for a second and said, "If God is as kind and gracious as you claim, then I'd rather take my chances living my life my way. I don't need a middleman telling me how to connect to Him."

She didn't say much after that.

That was the moment I realized I wasn't afraid anymore. I wasn't angry, either. I just didn't need anyone to translate love for me anymore.

That freedom, that breath, was the real beginning of growth.

There is the part of healing no one prepares you for. I call it the in-between. The space where the old version of you has died, but the new version hasn't quite formed yet. It's lonely. It's strange. It feels like standing in an empty house after the movers have left. Echoing and unfamiliar, but full of possibility.

You start noticing who disappears when your light changes, and who quietly steps forward. You learn that not everyone is meant to go with you, and that's okay. Some people loved the version of you who apologized for existing. They don't know what to do with the one who finally stands up straight.

Growth is messy. It doesn't come with applause. It comes with endings, grief, and an absurd number of days spent wondering if you've completely lost your mind.

I came close to that edge. There were nights I didn't recognize myself. The silence was deafening. The loneliness was thick. I felt like a shell of a person, stripped of everything that used to define me.

Then came the night I truly broke.

It wasn't dramatic. There was no music swelling in the background, no Hollywood epiphany. Just me on the cold kitchen floor, tears streaming down my face, whispering to no one in particular, *I can't do this anymore.*

Ken didn't rush in to fix it. He didn't feed me clichés or tell me to look on the bright side. He quietly made a cup of tea, then sat down next to me. Not across the room. Not hovering awkwardly. Right there on the floor, in the mess, in the quiet.

He didn't talk. He didn't need to. He just sat there until my breathing slowed.

That's when I learned something about love, real love. It doesn't always speak; it holds space. It doesn't rescue you; it reminds you you're not alone.

That moment changed everything. Because it showed me that even though I'd fallen apart, I hadn't failed. I was exactly where I needed to be, stripped down, raw, and finally real.

That's what growth looks like. It's not tidy. It's not spiritual Instagram quotes and positive affirmations. It's gut-level honesty and surrender. It's shaking, crying, and still choosing to get up the next morning.

And slowly, quietly, something began to rebuild.

Not the old version of me (she was gone, and thank God for that) but a softer, wiser, truer version began to take her place. The version that didn't need everyone's approval. The version that could say "no" without apology. The version that could finally look in the mirror and see a woman who had survived herself.

Ken was there through all of it, not as my savior, but as my witness. He watched me fall apart and never once made me feel ashamed for it. And in that, I found something sacred. The realization that love isn't supposed to save you; it's supposed to *see* you.

My first marriage broke me open. My second one taught me how to stay open without falling apart.

Growth often disguises itself as destruction. You lose things, people, and parts of yourself you thought you needed, only to realize they were never meant to stay.

It's brutal. It's beautiful. It's real.

And one day, you wake up and realize that the version of you who thought she couldn't survive… did.

And that's when you understand the strange mercy of it all — that every heartbreak, every unraveling, every goodbye was not a punishment, but preparation. The Universe didn't ignore your prayers. It just waited until you were strong enough to answer them yourself. Leaving the church wasn't the end of my faith. It was the beginning of trust, not in institutions, but in timing. And maybe that's the real miracle of growth. Realizing that freedom doesn't come when life finally gets easy. It comes the moment you decide to breathe on your own.

Chapter 6 – Divine and Terrible Timing

Because apparently, the Universe doesn't care about your calendar.

I used to think I could control everything in my world.

If I could plan it, predict it, and prepare for it, then nothing bad could happen, right? I had color-coded calendars, backup plans for my backup plans, and a deep belief that being prepared meant being protected. Control wasn't just a comfort; it was my false sense of safety.

Then life, with its impeccable comedic timing, said, "That's adorable. Watch this."

Because if there's one thing I've learned, it's that the Universe runs on its own clock. And it doesn't check with yours first.

You can plan, pray, journal, manifest, and white-knuckle your way through life, but when the timing isn't right, nothing moves. And when it *is* right, it'll happen so fast you won't even have time to second-guess it.

Divine timing is beautiful in hindsight and infuriating in real time.

There have been moments in my life where I was convinced the Universe had completely forgotten about me. When jobs fell through, when money was tight, when relationships ended, I'd find myself screaming inside, *Why now? Why me? Why can't this one thing just work out?*

It's a very human question, but one the Universe tends to answer with silence and irony.

I remember one particular "perfectly timed" disaster. A few years back, I was up for a job that seemed ideal. The kind that checked all the boxes and promised stability after months of uncertainty. I nailed the interview, felt confident, and was already mentally spending the first paycheck.

Then I got the email: "We've decided to move in another direction."

That direction, apparently, did not include me.

I was crushed. I needed that job. I had bills due and a rapidly diminishing faith in humanity. I remember sitting at my kitchen table, rereading that email like maybe the words would rearrange themselves into "Just kidding!"

A few weeks later, Ken got an unexpected opportunity in another city. A position that would move us to a new place and completely change the trajectory of our lives.

When he accepted it, I felt two things at once, scared and excited. Scared because it meant leaving behind everything familiar, and excited because deep down, I knew the Universe had just cracked open the next chapter for us. I also knew that our lives would never be the same again.

It's funny how fear and faith often sound identical at first; your heart pounding, your stomach flipping, your mind whispering, *What if this is it?* You don't know if you're standing on the edge of disaster or destiny until you take the leap.

If I'd gotten that original job, we never would've moved. And if we never would've moved, I wouldn't be sitting here writing this book surrounded by mountains, chickens, and peace I didn't even know I needed.

That job rejection felt like failure at the time. Now I see it as divine rerouting.

That's the tricky part about divine timing. It rarely feels divine when you're in it. It feels inconvenient, cruel, even unfair. But what I've come to realize is that divine timing isn't about punishment. It's about alignment.

The Universe isn't out to delay your dreams. It's trying to deliver them when you're actually ready to receive them.

It took me years to stop asking "Why me?" and start asking "What is this trying to teach me?"

That small shift changed everything. Because when you stop taking every disappointment personally, you start seeing the pattern underneath it. You start noticing how every closed door redirected you somewhere better, even if it took a while to understand it.

Every heartbreak softened me. Every delay taught me patience. Every loss stripped away something I didn't need. Every detour delivered me to something I couldn't have found if I'd gotten my way.

And let's be honest, sometimes the Universe's timing just sucks. You can be sitting in a mess thinking, *There's no way this could ever lead anywhere good,* and then one random Tuesday, you realize it was all setting you up for something bigger.

These days, when plans fall apart, I try (and usually fail at first) to breathe instead of panic. I remind myself that maybe it's not rejection, it's protection. Maybe what I wanted wasn't bad, it just wasn't *right now.*

Now, when things don't go according to my plan, I try to laugh. Because if there's one thing the Universe loves, it's proving me wrong with a sense of humor.

So when life goes sideways, I don't ask "Why me?" anymore. I just mutter, "Okay, Universe. I see you. Let's get this over with."

And somehow, it always works out. Rarely on time, but always on purpose.

And that's the heart of divine timing. It's never about getting what you want when you want it. It's about learning to trust the pauses. Faith isn't knowing how it ends, it's moving anyway. It's packing the boxes, taking the job, following the nudge, even when your voice shakes. Every great change in my life has started with that same cocktail of fear and excitement. Proof that the Universe doesn't just redirect you; it invites you forward. And the moment you say *yes,* everything that once terrified you begins to make perfect sense.

Chapter 7 – The Universe Doesn't Speak in Billboards (But Probably Should)

Because apparently, divine messages come with humor.

I used to think the Universe spoke in signs so obvious they'd be impossible to miss. You know, a flash of lightning, a booming voice, a cosmic text message that said, *"Hey, Katie, this way."*

Turns out, it's usually quieter than that. It speaks through gut feelings, coincidences, the right person showing up at the right moment, or a tractor part that breaks down for no reason — delaying you just long enough to avoid something worse. (Ask Ken. He's unintentionally on the Universe's payroll when it comes to divine timing through mechanical failure.)

But lately, I've started to realize something deeper. Maybe it's not just that the Universe sends signs *to* us. Maybe it speaks *through* us.

We all come into this life with certain spiritual gifts. Ever wonder why some people are born with voices that can stop you mid-sentence? Or hands that seem to heal, create, or build like they've done it for centuries? Why some people can read a room, sense danger, or know exactly what someone needs without being told?

Those aren't coincidences. Those are gifts.

I've come to believe that every soul carries specific abilities. Not just hobbies or talents, but sacred wiring that shapes what we're here to do and how we're meant to move through the world. Maybe you're an artist who translates emotion into color. Maybe you're a teacher who speaks light into dark places. Maybe you're a surgeon who can steady your hands when everyone else is trembling.

These aren't accidents. They're assignments.

Each of us has something. That one thing we can't *not* do, the thing that feels like breathing when we finally allow it. And when we use that gift, when we stop fighting or doubting it, something divine flows through us. It's not about ego. It's about alignment.

People like to talk about "gut instinct" as though it's just biology; a primal reaction left over from our cave-dwelling ancestors. But if you've ever felt that electric jolt in your stomach telling you something isn't right, or that warm certainty that something *is*, you know it's more than that.

That instinct, that knowing, is one of the most overlooked spiritual gifts there is.

It's the voice of your higher self, the thread that connects you to the divine, quietly whispering *this way*. It's not loud because it doesn't need to be. It already knows you're listening; or at least, that you could be, if you'd just slow down long enough to hear it.

Gut instinct keeps us safe. It steers us toward what's right for us and away from what isn't. It's saved me more times than I can count. From dangerous situations, toxic people, and more than one poorly timed "great idea" that would've gone up in flames.

And yet, for most of my life, I was taught to ignore it.

To defer to authority.

To silence my intuition because "God doesn't speak that way." Or worse yet, to say those feelings were from the devil.

The irony is, that *was* God speaking.

I think the Universe — God, Source, whatever name feels right — speaks in ways that match the tools it gave you. Some people hear, some see, some feel, some just *know*. None of it is random.

It's like a divine fingerprint; unique to you, impossible to duplicate.

Once you start honoring it, everything shifts. Life starts to feel less like guessing and more like remembering. Decisions come easier. The noise quiets. The path doesn't always make sense, but it feels right, and that's enough.

Ken, of course, doesn't use the word *intuition*. He calls it "common sense." But even he'll admit there have been moments when logic couldn't explain what happened, when he just "had a feeling" to stop, to wait, to turn around.

Like the time a piece of equipment broke down on the farm right before a major storm hit. If it hadn't failed, he would've been out in the middle of nowhere with no cell signal when it hit. Instead, he was safe in the shop, muttering about parts while the wind howled outside.

Coincidence? Maybe.

But I've learned to stop arguing with small miracles.

Because sometimes the Universe doesn't need to shout.

Sometimes it just delays your tractor.

What I love most about recognizing these gifts is how ordinary they seem. We expect divine power to look like lightning bolts and angels. But what if it's actually subtle; a song lyric that hits you at the exact right moment, a friend who calls out of nowhere, a sentence in a book that changes your whole outlook?

We miss so many messages because we're looking for billboards when the guidance is already built into us.

The Universe doesn't hide truth; it hides it *in plain sight.*
In our passions.
Our instincts.
Our gifts.

That's why your purpose isn't something you have to chase down. It's something you uncover by paying attention to what makes you feel alive.

If you've ever felt like you're waiting for permission to use your gifts, here it is: *You already have it.* The divine didn't put those abilities in you by accident. You came here with them on purpose.

Your intuition, your creativity, your empathy — those aren't random personality traits. They're the language of the Universe speaking through you. And every time you use them, you become the message someone else was waiting for.

And maybe that's the point we keep forgetting. That our "spiritual gifts" aren't something we earn or discover; they're something we remember. They're proof that we've never been disconnected, just distracted. Every instinct, every spark of creativity, every quiet nudge is the Universe reminding us, *You already know the way.*

All you have to do is trust the voice that's been with you since the beginning.

Chapter 8 – Faith Without the Fine Print

Rewriting what it means to believe.

For most of my life, I thought faith meant obedience. The stricter the rule, the holier the result. If I followed every command, every guideline, every ridiculous restriction to the letter, I would stay in God's good graces. Or at least out of His wrath.

That's not faith. That's control with a halo on it.

My old religion had a rule for everything. No coffee. No tea. No R-rated movies. No tank tops. No reading of "unapproved" materials because apparently God could create the heavens and the earth but not handle me reading a book He didn't sign off on.

The list went on forever. And the message was clear; if it brought joy, comfort, or individuality, it was probably off-limits.

I used to obey it all. Not because I agreed, but because I was terrified. They'd convinced me that faith was a tightrope, and one wrong step meant eternal damnation. So, I tiptoed through life trying not to anger a God I was told loved me unconditionally, just, you know, conditionally.

When you're living inside a box, sooner or later, you start running out of air.

My rebellion wasn't loud or dramatic, it started small. One Sunday, I did the unthinkable, I went to the grocery store. Sunday shopping was strictly forbidden, but I needed milk, and I was tired of waiting for Monday to roll around.

49

As I pushed my cart down the aisle, I half expected lightning to strike the produce section. I figured at minimum, my car wouldn't start when I got home. But nothing happened. The earth didn't split open. My soul didn't combust. The bananas even looked especially ripe.

It was almost disappointing.

That's when it hit me. All that fear, all those restrictions, all that guilt, it wasn't God. It was people pretending to speak for Him.

True faith, I realized, doesn't need to micromanage your grocery list.

That was the beginning of my spiritual freedom; not from God, but from the noise that kept me from hearing Him. I started questioning everything I'd been told was "sinful." Coffee? Delicious. Tank tops? Comfortable. R-rated movies? Some of them are cinematic masterpieces.

And the world didn't end.

Faith, as it turns out, has nothing to do with fear. It's not about rule-following or blind obedience. It's about trust. Trust in yourself, trust in love, trust that the Universe isn't waiting to smite you for being human.

When I stopped treating God like an angry supervisor and started seeing the divine as a loving partner in my life, everything changed. My prayers stopped sounding like desperate job interviews and started sounding like real conversations.

Now, my faith looks nothing like it used to. It's messy, it's personal, and it doesn't come with a checklist. Some days, I talk to the Universe over coffee, which I now drink proudly. Some days, I'm quiet and still. Some days, I'm angry or lost or laughing hysterically at the absurdity of it all.

And yet, in all of it, I feel connected.

Because real faith doesn't demand perfection. It invites presence. It doesn't cage you with conditions. It sets you free.

The moment I stopped trying to earn divine approval, I realized I'd had it all along.

And no, I haven't self-destructed yet. I've just learned to live.

Maybe that's what faith without the fine print really is. Remembering that you were never meant to prove your worth to the divine. You were meant to experience it. To live, to laugh, to doubt, to trust, to spill coffee on your own rulebook and still know, deep down, that you're loved beyond measure.

That's not rebellion. That's freedom.

Chapter 9 – Faith Before We Could Spell It

Because if Mom says it's true, it must be, right?

How ironic is it that we spend half our lives trying to "find faith," when the truth is, it was handed to us long before we could even spell it. Before the rules, before the guilt, before we learned to fear getting it wrong. Somewhere along the way, we traded instinct for instruction. But faith, real, breathing, human faith, starts much earlier than that. It starts in the stories we were told, the ones that taught us who God was, long before we were old enough to ask who we might be without Him.

Religion doesn't just happen to us as adults. It's planted early, long before we can read, drive, or decide if broccoli is edible. It comes wrapped in bedtime prayers, Sunday routines, and parental certainty. Before you even know what you believe, someone's already telling you who God likes, what He hates, and exactly how disappointed He'll be if you don't behave.

In the religion I grew up in, we had something called Testimony Sunday once a month. Picture an open mic night for spiritual one-upmanship. Members would line up at the pulpit to "bear their testimonies," declaring that our church was *the one true church* and everyone else was, well, politely wrong.

It was supposed to be a sacred, heartfelt experience. Sometimes it was. Other times, it was like listening to the same speech on repeat with different hairstyles. "I know this church is true." "I know so-and-so is the true prophet." "I know our leaders will never lead us astray."

I sat there, month after month, hearing the same script and watching small children, barely out of diapers, being lifted onto the podium to repeat it. Their mothers would crouch down beside them, whispering each line in their ear while the congregation smiled, misty-eyed, at this "sweet moment of faith."

I remember thinking, *That kid still eats crayons.* How in the world could he "know" eternal truth when he can't even tie his shoes?

But that's the point, isn't it? We don't *know,* we're taught to *recite.* We mistake memorization for conviction. By the time we're old enough to think critically, the belief is already welded to our identity. To question it feels like betraying not just God, but family.

That's how it sticks.

We grow up thinking, *It must be true — my parents said so, my teachers said so, everyone I love believes it, so who am I to question it?* It's not brainwashing in the cartoon-villain sense. It's gentler, subtler. It's bedtime stories and community potlucks and promises of forever families. It's belonging, until it's not.

And make no mistake, it works. Because kids want approval more than they want truth. We'll believe whatever makes Mom smile and Dad proud. So when the message is *"You're good when you obey and bad when you doubt,"* it burrows deep.

By the time you're grown, you don't need anyone to tell you what to believe, you tell yourself. The voice that once belonged to your parents becomes your own inner critic. You self-correct, self-censor, self-shame. That's the genius of conditioning. Eventually, it runs on autopilot.

I didn't see it clearly until I had kids of my own. One day, watching a mother at church prompt her toddler to the microphone, I felt this pang in my chest, a mix of nostalgia and nausea. The little girl lisped out, "I know this church is true," and the whole room melted with pride. And all I could think was, *No, sweetheart. You just know the words. The meaning comes later — if they ever let you find it for yourself.*

That moment opened something in me. Because I realized I wasn't angry at the people, I was angry at the system that made sincerity indistinguishable from indoctrination. The adults weren't evil; they were repeating what had been done to them. They believed they were giving their children safety. In reality, they were giving them certainty; a much smaller, heavier gift.

Children are supposed to believe in magic. They're supposed to think the tooth fairy and Santa and God are all on the same team. The problem is, religion doesn't always grow up when we do. It stays frozen in that same childhood logic, *my parents said it, my church said it, so it must be true.*

But the world isn't that simple. And neither is faith.

As adults, we have to go back and untangle what was ours from what was planted. We have to ask the questions we weren't allowed to as kids:

- Do I still believe this, or do I just fear what happens if I don't?
- Is my faith alive, or is it just inherited?
- And if I were raised somewhere else, would my "truth" look exactly the same?

Those are uncomfortable questions. But they're the kind that make your faith *real*, not recycled.

I used to think doubt was a flaw. Now I think it's the most honest form of faith there is. Because faith without choice isn't faith; it's programming.

And unlearning programming? That's holy work.

So when I think about those little kids at the pulpit now, parroting beliefs they don't understand, I don't judge them. I just hope one day, when they're old enough to stop eating dirt, they also get brave enough to taste the truth for themselves.

And maybe that's the quiet redemption of it all. That the faith we were given as children was never the problem. It was the fear we were taught to attach to it. Somewhere under the memorized lines and the conditioned obedience, that childlike trust still lives inside us, curious, innocent, unafraid to wonder. Real faith isn't something we lose when we grow up. It's something we reclaim when we finally remember what love, unfiltered by fear, was always trying to say.

Chapter 10 – The Gospel According to Good Girls

How to shrink yourself and call it salvation.

Growing up in the church as a young woman came with a very clear syllabus.

Be kind. Be pure. Be pretty but not distracting. Be quiet but always smiling.

And most importantly, *get married and procreate as fast as humanly possible.*

That was the goal.

Not college, not a career, not a dream beyond domestic bliss.

Your divine purpose was to become a wife and a mother. Period.

It wasn't said with cruelty. It was said with certainty. The women who taught me believed it with every fiber of their being. They'd smile and say things like, "The most important work you'll ever do will be within the walls of your own home." And as a kid, I believed them. Why wouldn't I? These were the women I admired. The ones with casseroles, perfectly curled bangs, and an endless ability to smile through exhaustion.

But somewhere deep down, I always had questions. Why didn't we ever talk about women becoming doctors, or lawyers, or CEOs? Why were the lessons always about modesty, homemaking, and "supporting your husband's priesthood"?

The message was clear; men were leaders, women were helpers. And if you were too loud, too curious, too ambitious, you were "worldly."

God forbid you wanted more than motherhood. That was arrogance, pride, or worse because you were not living appropriately.

And then there was the holy grail of all goals: marrying a returned missionary. A man who had served two years proclaiming the gospel, knocking on doors, and saving souls. The church called it "a badge of honor." In reality, it was a stamp of approval.

You could be a wonderful young woman, faithful, pure, devoted. But if your future husband hadn't served a mission, it was like buying a house without a foundation. People would *smile*, but they'd whisper.

I once asked my cousin why it mattered so much. She didn't hesitate. She said, "Because marrying a returned missionary is the only way to reach the highest level of heaven. You want to be with your family forever, don't you?"

Ah yes, *families are forever.* The slogan of eternal guilt.

I've met families.
Have you met families?

They're complicated, messy, and often mean. Some are loving, yes but plenty are manipulative, controlling, or outright abusive. And yet, the church taught us that the ultimate reward was to be sealed to those same people *for all eternity.*

Forever.

With the people who already made you feel small in this lifetime.

Gross.

The older I got, the more absurd it sounded. Can you imagine being told that you were eternally attached to someone who raped you, beat you, or emotionally destroyed you — forever? That you'd have to spend eternity "forgiving" and "enduring" alongside the very person who broke you?

I asked that question once, out loud. I wanted to know how heaven could possibly feel heavenly if it included abusers. Like everything else, the answer was a careful dance around the truth. Something about "God's plan" and "everyone being made whole again." It was a polished way of saying, *Don't ask questions you're not supposed to ask.*

If your version of heaven includes forcing victims to sit next to their abusers for eternity, it's not heaven. It's hell with better lighting.

When my family chose not to have me sealed to them for all eternity, that sent a cruel message straight to my heart. I was devastated.

You want to talk about feeling hurt? That was a special kind of pain. The kind that seeps in quietly and whispers, *You don't belong.*

I remember seeing the photos and thinking, *So much for unconditional love.* The message was loud and clear. Family is forever, but only if you follow the rules. Apparently, divine love has attendance requirements.

This also confirmed to me that this religious organization and its doctrine and rituals were a complete and utter joke. I came to realize that there was a difference between the God that created man and the man that attempted to create God.

I finally saw how far apart church "good" and real "good" actually were.

Church "good" was about appearances — clean-cut men, smiling women, perfect families who looked holy on paper. Real "good" is about kindness, empathy, and accountability — things that never seemed to make the Sunday lesson plan.

Inside the church, love was a transaction. Be obedient, stay loyal, toe the line, and you'll be rewarded with eternity together. Step out of line, and suddenly forever has a gate code you don't know.

I used to feel jealous, like I'd been left out of something sacred. Now, I'm grateful I wasn't sealed to people who only know how to love conditionally. If eternity is just an endless rerun of emotional manipulation and quiet resentment, I'll happily pass.

Because family, real family, isn't about ceremonies or signatures. It's about showing up, consistently, honestly, and without judgment. It's about the people who choose you over and over again, not because they're commanded to, but because they *want* to.

The church taught me that "forever family" was the ultimate goal. The Universe taught me that forever isn't about bloodlines or blessings, it's about connection.

I used to think I was missing out. Now I see that I was being spared.

And maybe that's the biggest lesson in all of it. That love without freedom isn't love. And faith without honesty isn't faith. I no longer believe in a heaven that rewards hierarchy or punishes independence. My idea of eternity looks a lot more like laughter around a fire, peace in my chest, and the quiet knowing that the people I love, truly love, will always find me, no sealing ceremony required.

And once you start asking those questions, the kind that poke holes in the picture-perfect version of heaven, you start seeing the cracks everywhere else, too. Because the same system that tells you who you're allowed to love also decides who's allowed to lead. It hands ordinary men sacred authority and calls it divine order. And just like that, control gets rebranded as holiness.

Chapter 11 – When Power Dresses Up as Holiness

The divine was never the problem. The people who built the stage were.

I've always wondered why smart, capable, educated people — people who read, question, and think critically — still get pulled into religion's grip. I used to think it was ignorance, until I realized I was one of them. I wasn't stupid. I wasn't naïve. I was just tired. And control, when you're exhausted or broken, can feel an awful lot like comfort.

Religion doesn't just offer belief; it offers structure. It gives you a checklist, a leader, and a promise that if you just follow directions, you'll be okay. For people like me, people who love a plan, a system, a little gold star for doing it "right." It's seductive.

That's what I think draws intelligent people in. Not stupidity. Not gullibility. Control disguised as clarity.

Power never shows up wearing horns. It shows up smiling, quoting scripture, and promising to lead you to the light. It talks about humility and service while quietly rearranging the furniture so it always sits at the head of the table.

The funny thing about organized religion is that it usually starts beautifully. A group of people experience something sacred, and they want to share it. They build a community, create rituals, write down some guidelines, and before long, someone says, *"We should probably have a leader."*

And that's when things start to slide.

Because the moment someone claims to *speak for God*, a committee forms to decide who's allowed to question them.

At first, it feels harmless. Leaders organize potlucks, visit the sick, make you feel like you belong. But slowly, quietly, the line between guidance and control starts to blur. The message shifts from "Here's what might help your soul" to "Here's what happens if you disobey."

And that's how love grows teeth.

I remember sitting in a church classroom one Sunday surrounded by bright, thoughtful people — teachers, nurses, accountants, people who should've known better — and nodding along while a man with zero counseling credentials confidently told us that depression was not a medical diagnosis but "a lack of faith."

I wanted to raise my hand and say, *"That's not how medicine works,"* but I didn't. I smiled. I nodded. And afterward, I sat in my car, hands gripping the steering wheel, fighting that rising heat in my chest that felt a lot like rage.

That moment was the beginning of my unraveling. Because it wasn't just about religion — it was about realizing how easily smart people trade discernment for belonging. That's the part that stings the most. I wasn't tricked. I was tired. I wanted to be told I was good, safe, worthy. And for a while, the rules gave me that illusion.

The truth is, power loves structure. It loves hierarchy and titles and the illusion of "special access." It loves being the gatekeeper between you and the divine because that's how it stays relevant. It whispers, *You can't trust your own intuition, come to me instead.* And we believe it, because we've been taught to confuse authority with wisdom.

My own experience with bishops was dismal at best. They were all just men acting on behalf of a God they barely understood. And when anyone — okay, *me* — dared to question them, I was rebuked for "lacking faith."

I was actually told by one bishop that the abuse I'd suffered in my marriage was justified because I "talked back" and "didn't honor my husband's priesthood." Think about that for a minute. Because I dared to question, it was okay to abuse me?

I sat there in his office, numb, staring at the man who claimed to speak for God while defending my abuser. That was the moment I realized that this wasn't about divinity at all. It was about men protecting men and calling it righteousness.

And it wasn't an isolated experience.

I remember sitting in a Sunday school meeting once where the stake president (the man above the bishops) came to lecture everyone on faith and obedience. He told us, in no uncertain terms, that as wives, if we questioned our husbands, we were not being faithful. That husbands were the priesthood leaders of the home and we were to follow — *at all costs.*

I looked around the room and saw nodding heads, tearful eyes, and women writing notes like they were receiving divine instruction. I didn't feel inspired. I felt sick. Not because I wasn't faithful, but because I couldn't believe these people actually bought this nonsense.

They weren't just worshipping God, they were worshipping hierarchy.

That day, I stopped wondering why so many women were miserable and started realizing why so many stayed that way. When you teach people that submission is salvation, you don't need to chain them, they'll lock the door themselves.

Eventually, fear becomes the currency.
"Stay faithful or lose your blessings."
"Obey your leaders or risk your salvation."
"Question anything, and you're spiritually unsafe."

It's spiritual blackmail dressed up as devotion.

The congregation doesn't realize what's happening. You just start shrinking; one compromise, one silence, one apologetic smile at a time. You stop trusting your gut because they've told you your gut is sinful. You stop asking questions because questions make them nervous. And eventually, the cage starts to feel like safety.

That's the trap of religious power. It doesn't need to chase you. It convinces you to lock the door from the inside.

When I finally walked away, the silence was deafening. No one telling me what to think, what to wear, or who to love. For the first time, I could breathe, and it scared the hell out of me. Because freedom and loneliness sound the same at first.

That's when I learned how deep the programming ran. The fear of being wrong. The reflex to seek approval. The guilt for choosing peace over punishment. It's like spiritual detox; you shake, you sweat, and then one day you wake up and realize the noise in your head isn't God. It's conditioning.

Looking back, I don't hate the people who led me. I understand them now. Power feels a lot like love when you're afraid of being irrelevant. Maybe that's why they cling to it. Maybe that's why I did too.

But I wish someone had told me years ago that divine love and power don't mix well. Love liberates. Power controls. Love invites. Power dictates. You can't serve both.

When religion and power fall in love, they create hierarchy. When love and humility fall in love, they create freedom.

I used to think questioning authority was dangerous. Now I think blind obedience is dangerous. Because any system that punishes curiosity isn't protecting your soul; it's protecting its structure.

And here's the irony. The same people who use fear to keep others small are terrified themselves. Terrified of losing control, losing followers, losing the illusion that they're closer to God than everyone else. Power doesn't just corrupt the followers; it imprisons the leaders too.

Every spiritual empire collapses under its own ego. Truth doesn't need defending, and love doesn't require loyalty oaths. The moment someone tells you salvation depends on obedience to *them,* you're not in faith, you're in a franchise.

The Divine doesn't need middle management.

Holiness isn't found in hierarchy; it's found in humility. It's that quiet knowing that no one owns the pathway to God, because the pathway runs straight through every one of us.

When I stopped chasing approval from people who claimed divine authority, I finally felt something real — peace. Not the kind that comes from being right, but the kind that comes from being free.

Organized religion doesn't attract bad people. It attracts people who crave certainty in an uncertain world. But when certainty becomes more important than compassion, power stops serving God and starts serving itself.

And maybe that's the final lesson. Faith isn't about being certain. It's about being honest enough to admit when you're not and still choosing love anyway.

For the longest time, I believed holiness lived in the hands of men who held titles. Now I know it lives quietly inside every one of us; in intuition, integrity, and courage. The divine doesn't need spokesmen; it needs listeners. Every time I trust my own knowing over someone else's authority, I return a little closer to myself. And maybe that's what real faith is. Not obedience to power, but remembrance of the truth you were born with.

Once you see the machinery of control for what it is, you'd think walking away would be easy. It's not. Because power doesn't just live in pulpits or church offices. It lives in your head long after you leave the building. It's in the guilt that follows you home, the reflex to apologize for thinking differently, the whisper that says you'll never be safe outside the system.

That's how power sustains itself, by teaching you to police yourself. You don't need the bishop anymore; you've internalized his voice. You second-guess your worth, your intuition, even your happiness, because somewhere along the line, you were told those things only exist under their approval.

Freedom sounds beautiful, but it comes with withdrawal. And that's what the next chapter is about. How control doesn't always end when the door closes behind you. Sometimes, it lingers inside you, pretending to be faith.

Chapter 12 – When Power Becomes Entrapment

Fear is the leash, not the lesson.

Once you walk away from religious control, you expect the chains to fall off. You expect freedom to feel like sunlight; bright, clean, instant relief. But that's not what happens.

Because power doesn't just hold you while you're there; it follows you when you leave.

It lingers in your thoughts, in your guilt, in that quiet, trembling fear that maybe they were right. That voice that whispers, *What if you've gone too far? What if you're wrong? What if God really does turn His back now?*

That's the real entrapment.

It's not the sermons or the bishops anymore. It's the programming.

You don't need to sit in the pew to still hear their voices echo in your head. The fear of being "cast out of the light." The fear of "losing your salvation." The fear that you'll spend eternity alone, wandering the void because you refused to kneel.

Fear is the greatest currency religion ever invented. It keeps people small, quiet, and compliant. You can't question, because questioning might mean exile. You can't say no, because no might mean eternal punishment.

And when you *do* finally stand up and say, *"No more,"* the mask slips.

They stop smiling and start warning.
They tell you your salvation will be taken away.
Your blessings revoked.
Your name blotted out.

They say it like they're reading from a divine HR manual. As if God is just waiting by a big celestial filing cabinet, ready to shred your eternal paperwork because you didn't renew your obedience on time.

But really, how do they know this?

Because some "prophet" from back in the day claimed he had a hotline to heaven while hallucinating in the forest? Because somewhere along the way, one man's mystical camping trip became doctrine and the rest of us built our lives around it?

It's wild when you think about it. An entire religion built around the idea that one man's mystical camping trip turned into divine law — and we just went along with it for generations.

We gave these men, these self-proclaimed middlemen, the authority to define our eternity. They told us who was chosen, who was damned, and what boxes we had to check to earn love that was supposedly unconditional.

That's not spirituality. That's spiritual *extortion*.

Fear is the glue that keeps the whole system together.

If they can convince you that leaving equals damnation, you'll never actually leave — not fully. You might stop showing up physically, but mentally, you'll still be sitting in the same pew, terrified of disappointing a God you were told was already disappointed.

I've seen it over and over. People who walk away but still live like they're being watched. They censor their words, their joy, even their peace. Because what if the bishop was right? What if the prophet really *did* have special access? What if heaven's velvet rope list has their name crossed out in red ink?

That fear isn't faith. It's programming.
And it's designed to keep you dependent.

The irony is, the people preaching fear usually call it love. They'll tell you, *"We just don't want you to lose your place in the Kingdom."*
Translation: *We just don't want to face the cracks in our own certainty.*

Because if one person can walk away and still find peace, the whole illusion collapses. If you can leave and still feel loved, they can't control you anymore.

So they double down.
They tell the congregation you're "lost."
They warn others not to associate.
They whisper that you've been deceived by the devil, which is ironic, considering how similar their tactics are.

Leaving isn't the betrayal.
Staying silent when you know better is.

Power becomes entrapment when fear is disguised as faith. When love is conditional. When salvation is sold as a subscription plan you can't afford to cancel.

I used to think it was blasphemy to question the prophets. Now I think it's blasphemy *not to*.

Because if your God is as loving, wise, and all-knowing as you claim, He can handle a few follow-up questions.

And if He can't, then maybe He's not the problem; the salesmen are.

Fear will tell you you're lost.
Freedom will whisper, *You were never lost — you were loyal to the wrong voice.*

And the moment you realize that, the whole illusion falls apart. The fear doesn't vanish overnight, but it starts to fade. Slowly, quietly, you begin to trust the light in yourself more than the spotlight of the pulpit.

Because the divine was never about submission. It was about connection.

And connection doesn't require control.

That's the freedom they warned you about — not because it's dangerous, but because it's real.

For years, I thought the threat of losing salvation was what kept me safe. Now I see it was what kept me small. Fear was never sacred, it was strategy. And the moment I stopped mistaking fear for faith, everything opened. The voice I was taught to dread turned out to be my own; calm, wise, unshakable. That's what they were really afraid of. Because once you remember that the divine lives inside you, no one can hold your eternity hostage ever again.

It's funny, once you finally escape the fear factory, you expect life to hand you a halo and a fresh start. Instead, the Universe hands you chaos with a smirk and says, *"Now that you're free, let's see what you've learned."*

Because apparently, divine timing comes with a sense of humor.

You think enlightenment will look like soft music and serenity, but sometimes it looks like flat tires, missed signs, and lessons disguised as cosmic pranks. I swear the Universe doesn't speak in thunderclaps, it speaks in irony. The moment you say, "I'll never do that again," the test reappears wearing a different hat.

Healing is not all deep breathing and candles. Sometimes it's sarcasm and stubbornness and the Universe laughing from the back row.

And that's where the next part of this story begins.

Chapter 13 – So Where Do We Go from Here?

You're the author now.

After you deconstruct a belief system that ruled your life, there's a strange silence that follows. The noise is gone; the rules, the guilt, the endless pressure to measure up. But so is the structure that held everything together.

It's liberating and terrifying all at once.

Because once the voices of authority fade, a new one starts to whisper: *"Now what?"*

That's the question every recovering believer eventually faces. You've stepped out of the system, you've burned the old script and now you're standing in the blank space of your own becoming.

So where do we go from here?

We start by realizing something that took me years to understand. **You get to decide.**

You get to decide how to worship, or if you even want to.

You get to decide how to pray, or what prayer even looks like for you.

You get to decide what you believe, who you love, how you live, and what "holy" means in your own language.

You are allowed to rebuild your spirituality without supervision.

For years, I thought I needed permission to be at peace. I thought there was only one correct way to connect with the divine; the church way, the approved way, the right way.

But the truth is, the divine doesn't care about your method. It cares about your meaning. Your intention.

You can pray on a mountain, in a car, at a kitchen sink full of dishes, or half-asleep in bed. You can meditate, journal, sing, dance, cry, or curse under your breath. The Universe doesn't need fancy words, it just needs honesty.

Now, don't get me wrong.

This isn't a free pass to lose your mind and rob a bank. There are still consequences for choices — that's just called being human. But I genuinely believe the Universe wants us to live a happy, curious, *full* life.

Not a perfect one. A real one.

One where we laugh too loud, screw up, fall in love, learn hard lessons, and still wake up grateful that we get to try again tomorrow.

Because that's what this whole experience is. It's trying again.

I believe in past lives. I always have.
And honestly, it's the only thing that makes sense to me.

How could anyone learn everything in one lifetime? How could we possibly master forgiveness, courage, love, grief, compassion, boundaries, and joy all in one go? We can't.

So we come back. Again and again.

Each lifetime gives us new material. New stories, new wounds, new chances to grow. It's like the Universe saying, *"You didn't quite nail that one, but let's try it from another angle."*

Some lifetimes are for survival. Some are for softness. Some are for building empires or tearing down illusions.

And this one, the one we're living right now, might just be for remembering.

Remembering who you are when no one else is telling you who to be.

Remembering that freedom isn't rebellion; it's your birthright.

Remembering that you were never meant to be perfect; you were meant to evolve.

The Universe doesn't grade you. It grows you.

It doesn't demand obedience; it invites experience.

You're allowed to explore. To ask questions. To get it wrong and then try again. To believe one thing today and another tomorrow.

You're allowed to change your mind, to shift your path, to rewrite your story a thousand times if you need to.

That's the whole point of living. To experience everything, to taste the full range of being human, and to come out a little wiser, a little softer, a little more open each time.

Maybe heaven isn't some faraway kingdom with golden gates and matching outfits.

Maybe it's right here, in the moments when you feel aligned, alive, and fully yourself.

Maybe heaven is just peace with who you are.

So where do we go from here?

Forward.

One imperfect, miraculous day at a time.

You don't need a prophet or a pastor or a priest to tell you where to find God. You just have to live. You'll find the divine in laughter, in forgiveness, in starting over, in the quiet space between chaos and clarity.

Because maybe that's the real lesson. The Universe doesn't want blind followers, it wants conscious creators. And you, my friend, are one of them.

The funny thing about claiming your freedom is that the Universe immediately celebrates by throwing you a pop quiz. You finally declare, *"I'm at peace,"* and the next day your Wi-Fi dies, your car won't start, and your husband buys another tractor. Apparently, enlightenment comes with entertainment value. The Universe doesn't test you to punish you. It tests you to prove you're ready. And sometimes, it does it with a wicked grin. Because once you start living by your own rules, life stops being a sermon and starts being a stand-up routine. One where you're both the student and the punchline.

Chapter 14 – The Universe Has Jokes

The punchline was peace all along.

If you'd told me years ago that I'd one day sit here, at peace with my past, I would've laughed in your face. Not a polite laugh either. It would have been the kind that says, *"Bless your delusional heart."* Because back then, peace wasn't even on the horizon. Survival was.

I've walked through fire and not the poetic kind. The kind that scorches you from the inside out, that takes everything familiar and leaves you standing in the ashes wondering who you are now.

But here's what I've learned. The Universe has a wicked sense of humor, and somehow, it's always rooting for you.

It'll test you, trip you, tease you and just when you're ready to give up, it'll hand you a moment so beautiful it makes all the bruises make sense.

I've been through heartbreak, manipulation, divorce, excommunication, and more than one spiritual identity crisis. I've doubted everything, including myself. But every time I thought I was done, life had another chapter waiting. Not a punishment. A continuation.

The Universe never once said, *"You failed."*
It just said, *"Try again, but this time, as the real you."*

These days, I live slower. Softer. More aligned with the person I was always meant to be, the one buried under years of fear, expectation, and trying to be "good."

I still stumble. I still say the wrong thing, overthink, and occasionally let Ken talk me into projects that require duct tape and optimism. But now, my reactions come from a different place, not panic, but presence.

I used to believe life was about earning worthiness. Now I know it's about *remembering* it.

Every sunrise, every laugh, every quiet evening on the porch with Ken and a cup of coffee reminds me that peace isn't found in perfection, it's found in permission. Permission to be human. Permission to heal. Permission to start over as many times as it takes.

The Universe never promised easy. It promised *meaning*.

I look at the life I've built. The books I've written, the love, the chickens, the chaos, and I see proof that miracles don't always arrive in halos. Sometimes they wear work boots and call you "babe." Sometimes they look like second chances. Sometimes they sound like your own laughter after years of silence.

When you survive tremendous odds, you stop waiting for the light at the end of the tunnel and realize you were carrying it the whole damn time.

I'm still learning. I probably always will be. But now, my lessons don't come from fear, they come from faith in myself. My thought process, my intuition, my humor, my hope — all of it finally feels like home.

If you've made it this far, maybe you're walking your own path out of something that tried to shrink you. Maybe you're rebuilding, remembering, relearning how to trust yourself.

Here's what I want you to know:
You're doing it right.
You're not late.
You're not lost.
You're just becoming.

The Universe isn't keeping score; it's cheering you on.

And even when the road gets rough, and it will, you'll find small mercies tucked into the mess. A kind word. A warm sunrise. A laugh you didn't know you still had in you. Those are the Universe's love notes.

Life isn't about escaping the storm; it's about learning to dance in the rain and still notice the rainbow when it shows up. The Universe has jokes, yes, but they're never cruel. They're reminders that even when everything feels impossible, you're still exactly where you're meant to be.

So here's to the next chapter; yours, mine, and the ones we haven't written yet. May it be full of laughter, grace, and the quiet knowing that you've already survived the hardest parts.

And may you never forget the Universe doesn't laugh *at* you. It laughs *with* you because it already knows you're going to be just fine.

Epilogue – The Light We Carry Forward

Because the story doesn't end here — it just changes shape.

When I started writing this book, I didn't realize I was really writing my way home. Every chapter, every hard truth, every sarcastic punchline was me unpacking the boxes I'd been living in. The ones built by fear, obedience, and other people's definitions of who I was supposed to be.

If you're holding this book right now, you probably know what that feels like.
To unlearn what you were told was "holy."
To question what you were told was "truth."
To slowly realize that the divine isn't a rulebook, it's a relationship.

Somewhere along the way, I stopped trying to find God "out there" and started recognizing the divine in small, ordinary things. In coffee steam curling up toward the morning light. In the quiet hum of the farm. In the way Ken looks at me when I'm mid-rant and says, "You're not wrong." (That's love. Possibly survival.)

I didn't become enlightened — I became real.

And maybe that's what this whole journey was for.

To remember that spirituality isn't about perfection. It's about presence.

To learn that faith isn't about obedience. It's about trust.

To understand that peace isn't something you chase. It's something you allow.

When I think back on the version of me who was terrified to question, to doubt, to leave, I don't judge her anymore. She was doing her best with the tools she had. She wanted to belong, to be good, to be loved. What she didn't know yet was that belonging, goodness, and love were never something she had to earn.

If I could reach back and whisper in her ear, I'd tell her, "You're not walking away from God. You're walking toward yourself. And that's holy, too."

I don't have all the answers. Honestly, I don't think we're supposed to.

But I do know this. Every time you choose honesty over comfort, you evolve.

Every time you choose laughter over bitterness, you heal.

Every time you choose love — real, honest, no-strings-attached love — you become a little more like the light that made you.

That's what this book is about. Not religion. Not rebellion. Not even recovery.

It's about remembering. Remembering that the divine was never somewhere else. It was here, in you, the entire time.

If this book found you in a moment of searching, I hope it also leaves you in a moment of peace. Not the kind that comes from having it all figured out, but the kind that comes from realizing you don't have to.

You can rest now. You can breathe. You can laugh again. You can rebuild your faith, your life, your identity — one imperfect, glorious step at a time.

And when the Universe throws you another curveball (because it will), may you smile, roll your eyes, and say, "Alright, I get it. Nice one."

From My Heart to Yours

Thank you for walking with me through this story, my story. For listening without judgment, for laughing where I laughed, and for letting my chaos remind you of your own courage.

If there's one thing I hope you carry from these pages, it's this:
You are not broken.
You are not lost.
You are becoming.

And the world needs exactly *who you are* — not who you were told to be.

So go live. Go laugh. Go love wildly and freely and without apology.

Build your own damn table, live your own faith, and never forget that the Universe has a soft spot for stubborn hearts.

Because you made it here — through everything.

And that means, my friend, that you are already light.

A Note from the Author

If you've come to know me through *My Own Damn Table* or found your way here by chance, thank you for trusting me with your time and your heart.

This story, and every story I write, is proof that we can walk through hell and still come out with humor, grace, and a damn good story to tell.

I will continue to write stories, if nothing else to make you smile and know it's all going to be ok.

Until the next story, thank you for sitting at my table, again. Here's to all the lessons, laughter, and late-night talks still waiting for us.

With much love,

Katie

www.ingramcontent.com/pod-product-compliance
Lightning Source LLC
Chambersburg PA
CBHW070534130626
46555CB00003B/1413